Managing Editor
Ina Massler Levin, M.A.

Editor
Eric Migliaccio

Contributing Editor
Sarah Smith

Creative Director
Karen J. Goldfluss, M.S. Ed.

Cover Design
Tony Carrillo / Marilyn Goldberg

Teacher Created Resources, Inc.

6421 Industry Way
Westminster, CA 92683
www.teachercreated.com

ISBN: 978-1-4206-5930-6

© 2008 Teacher Created Resources, Inc.
Reprinted, 2009
Made in U.S.A.

This book belongs to

_____

Ready·Set·Learn

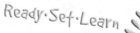

Get Ready to Learn!

Get ready, get set, and go! Boost your child's learning with this exciting series of books. Geared to help children practice and master many needed skills, the *Ready • Set • Learn* books are bursting with 64 pages of learning fun. Use these books for . . .

- ☀ enrichment
- ☀ skills reinforcement
- ☀ extra practice

With their smaller size, the *Ready • Set • Learn* books fit easily in children's hands, backpacks, and book bags. All your child needs to get started are pencils, crayons, and colored pencils.

A full sheet of colorful stickers is included. Use these stickers for . . .

- ☀ decorating pages
- ☀ rewarding outstanding effort
- ☀ keeping track of completed pages

Celebrate your child's progress by using these stickers on the reward chart located on the inside cover. The blue-ribbon sticker fits perfectly on the certificate on page 64.

With *Ready • Set • Learn* and a little encouragement, your child will be on the fast track to learning fun!

Word Problems #1

Directions: Write a number sentence for each story. Give the answer.

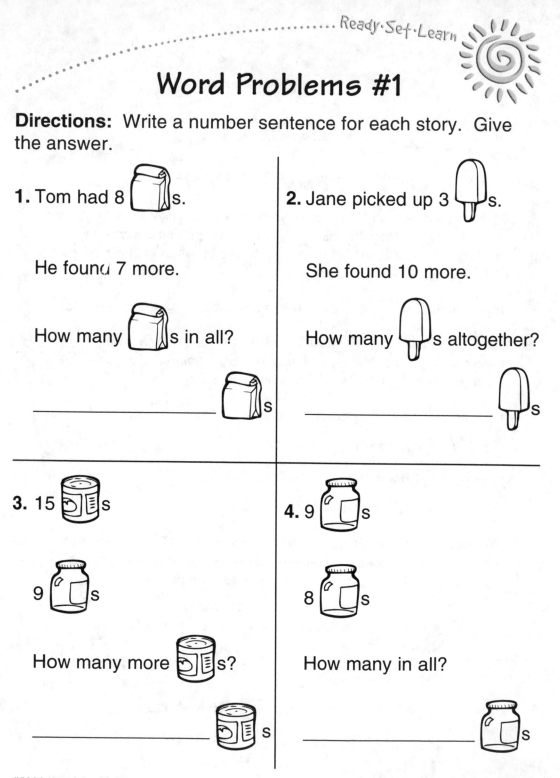

1. Tom had 8 ◻s.

He found 7 more.

How many ◻s in all?

_____ s

2. Jane picked up 3 ◻s.

She found 10 more.

How many ◻s altogether?

_____ s

3. 15 ◻s

9 ◻s

How many more ◻s?

_____ s

4. 9 ◻s

8 ◻s

How many in all?

_____ s

4

Word Problems #2

Directions: Solve the problems.

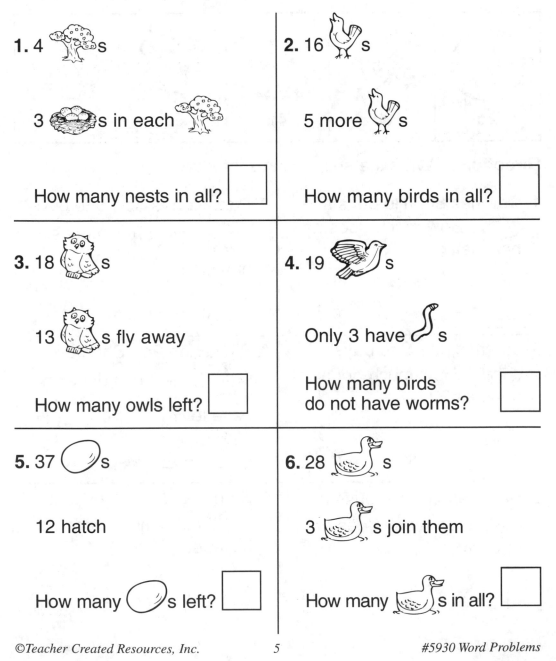

1. 4 🌳 s

3 🪺 s in each 🌳

How many nests in all? ☐

2. 16 🐔 s

5 more 🐦 s

How many birds in all? ☐

3. 18 🦉 s

13 🦉 s fly away

How many owls left? ☐

4. 19 🐦 s

Only 3 have 🪱 s

How many birds do not have worms? ☐

5. 37 🥚 s

12 hatch

How many 🥚 s left? ☐

6. 28 🦆 s

3 🦆 s join them

How many 🦆 s in all? ☐

Word Problems #3

Directions: Write the subtraction sentence.

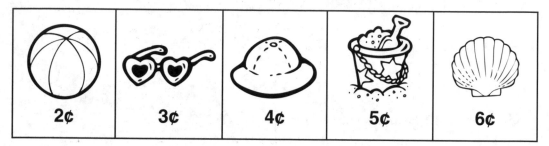

| 2¢ | 3¢ | 4¢ | 5¢ | 6¢ |

Directions: Write the subtraction sentence.

1. Dan has 8¢. He buys a ⬡. How much does he have left?

_____ ¢ − _____ ¢ = _____ ¢

2. Pamela has 5¢. She buys a 🪣. How much does she have left?

_____ ¢ − _____ ¢ = _____ ¢

3. Jan has 8¢. She buys 👓. How much does he have left?

_____ ¢ − _____ ¢ = _____ ¢

4. Stella has 9¢. She buys a 🪣. How much does she have left?

_____ ¢ − _____ ¢ = _____ ¢

5. Sam has 4¢. He buys a ⚪. How much does he have left?

_____ ¢ − _____ ¢ = _____ ¢

6. Stan has 7¢. He buys a 🐚. How much does he have left?

_____ ¢ − _____ ¢ = _____ ¢

Word Problems #4

1. Mom made 8 cookies. Sue ate 3.

How many cookies were left? _____

2. Pam baked 10 cookies. Ned took 4.

How many cookies did Pam have left? _____

3. Sid had 6 cookies. He gave 1 to Dan.

How many cookies did Sid have left? _____

4. Nan made 9 cookies. She ate 2.

How many cookies did she have left? _____

Word Problems #5

Directions: Solve the problems.

1. Cheryl has 5 marbles. Cindy has 2 more marbles than Cheryl. How many marbles does Cindy have?

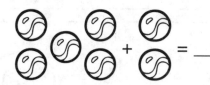

Cindy has _____ marbles.

2. Henry has 4 stamps. Eric has 5 more stamps than Henry. How many stamps does Eric have?

Eric has _____ stamps.

3. Gabby bought a piece gum. Bobby bought 3 more pieces of gum than Gabby. How many pieces of gum did Bobby buy?

Bobby bought _____ pieces of gum.

3. Ana has 1 puzzle. Deanna has 5 more puzzles than Ana. How many puzzles does Deanna have?

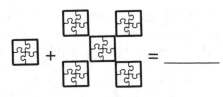

Deanna has _____ puzzles.

Word Problems #6

Directions: Solve the problems.

1. Marcy found 4 seeds in one pumpkin. She found 2 seeds in another pumpkin. How many seeds did Marcy find in all?

$Q\,Q\,Q\,Q + Q\,Q =$ _____

Marcy found _____ seeds in all.

2. Mark found 1 pumpkin seed in his pocket. He found 3 pumpkin seeds in his shoe. How many pumpkin seeds did Mark find in all?

$Q + Q\,Q\,Q =$ _____

Mark found _____ seeds in all.

3. Linda had 4 pumpkins. She bought 1 more. How many pumpkins does she have in all?

⊕ ⊕ ⊕ ⊕ + ⊕ = ___

4   **5**   **6**   **7**

4. Johnny found 4 pumpkins in the hay loft. He found 2 more in the hay wagon. How many pumpkins did he find in all?

⊕⊕ ⊕⊕ + ⊕⊕ = ___

5   **6**   **7**   **8**

Word Problems #7

Directions: Solve the problems.

1. My sister bought 1 apple. Then she bought 2 more. How many apples did she buy in all?

She bought _____ apples in all.

2. My brother had 2 apple pies. Then he bought 3 more apple pies. How many apple pies did he buy in all?

He bought _____ apple pies in all.

3. Jenna had 3 apples already. She picked 3 more off of her apple tree. How many apples does Jenna have in all?

She has_____ apples in all.

4. Carmine didn't have any apples. His friend Paulo gave him 1 apple. How many apples does Carmine have now?

$0 +$ 🍎 $=$ _____

Carmine has _____ apple in all.

Word Problems #8

1. I had 2 flowers and then picked 3 more. How many do I have? Draw the flowers and write the numbers.

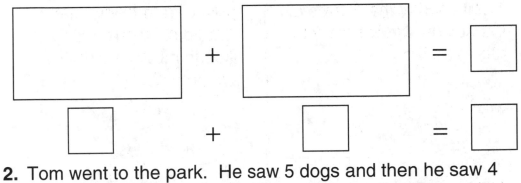

2. Tom went to the park. He saw 5 dogs and then he saw 4 more. How many dogs did he see? Draw the dogs and write the numbers.

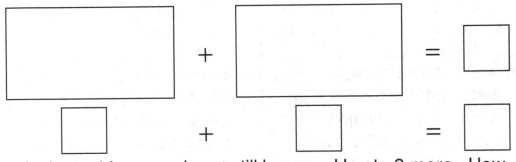

3. Jack ate 4 buns and was still hungry. He ate 3 more. How many did he eat? Draw the buns and write the numbers.

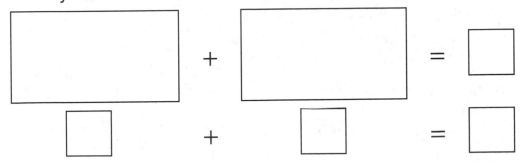

Word Problems #9

Directions: Solve the problems.

1. Billy saw 4 bats, and I saw 5 bats. How many bats did we see in all?

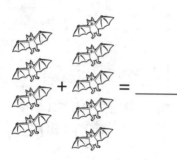

We saw _____ bats in all.

2. Susan saw 3 bats. Tasha saw 6 bats. How many bats did Susan and Tasha see in all?

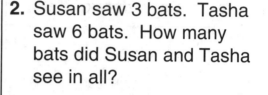

They saw _____ bats in all.

3. Aunt Clara once saw 5 fruit bats and 3 fish-eating bats. How many bats did Aunt Clara see in all?

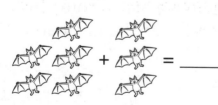

Aunt Clara saw _____ bats in all.

4. On Monday, Uncle Sean saw 5 brown bats. On Tuesday, he saw some more brown bats. He saw 10 bats in all. How many bats did he see on Tuesday?

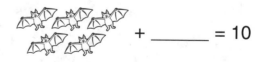

Uncle Sean saw _____ bats on Tuesday.

Word Problems #10

Directions: Solve the problems.

1. Sally put up 5 tents. Rob put up 2 tents. How many tents did they put up in all?

They put up _____ tents in all.

2. Zach saw 3 stars in the night sky. Rosie saw 6 stars. How many stars did they see in all?

They saw _____ stars in all.

3. Diego put up 2 tents in the first camp. Diego then put up 6 tents in the second camp. How many tents did Diego put up in all?

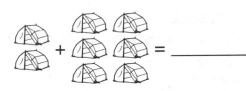

Diego put up _____ tents in all.

4. Emily found 1 rock while on her morning walk. She later found 8 rocks while on her evening walk. How many rocks did Emily find in all?

Emily found _____ rocks in all.

Word Problems #11

Directions: Solve the word problems below. Show your work with a number sentence or a picture on the right.

1. Tyler shoots 7 baskets. He misses 3 times. How many baskets did he make? _____	**Show Your Work**
2. Six children are playing hockey. Two children have to go home. How many children are left? _____	**Show Your Work**
3. There are five cookies on a plate. Mandi comes home from school and eats some. Now there are only two cookies on the plate. How many cookies did Mandi eat? _____	**Show Your Work**
4. Bernice's homework packet has 8 pages in it. She has completed 6 pages. How many more pages of homework does Bernice have to do? _____	**Show Your Work**

14

Word Problems #12

Directions: Solve the problems.

1. Ms. Grain had 8 turkeys on her farm. She sold 6 of the turkeys. How many turkeys does Ms. Grain have left?

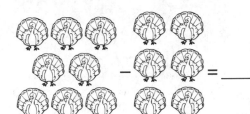

Ms. Grain has _____ turkeys left.

2. Nick collects turkey feathers. Yesterday he collected 7 turkey feathers. He dropped 4 of them on his way home. How many feathers does Nick have left?

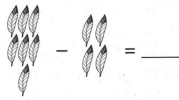

Nick has _____ turkey feathers left.

3. Omar saw 7 turkeys sitting on the gate. If 3 of the turkeys flew away, how many turkeys were left?

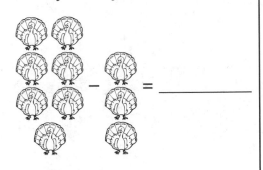

There were _____ turkeys left.

4. Vivian gave her pet turkey 9 ears of corn. The turkey ate 2 ears of corn. How many ears of corn are left?

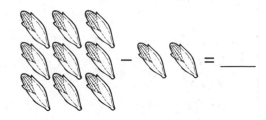

There are _____ ears left.

Word Problems #13

Directions: Solve the problems.

1. There are 8 chicks. If 2 run away, how many would be left?

There would be _____ chicks left.

2. There are 10 owls. If 9 fly away, how many are left?

There would be _____ owl left.

3. Noel saw 9 spiders in the hay loft. If 3 of them were not spinning webs, how many spiders were spinning webs?

There were _____ spiders spinning webs.

4. Tim has 9 ducks. If 2 ducks waddle away, how many ducks does Tim have left?

Tim has _____ ducks left.

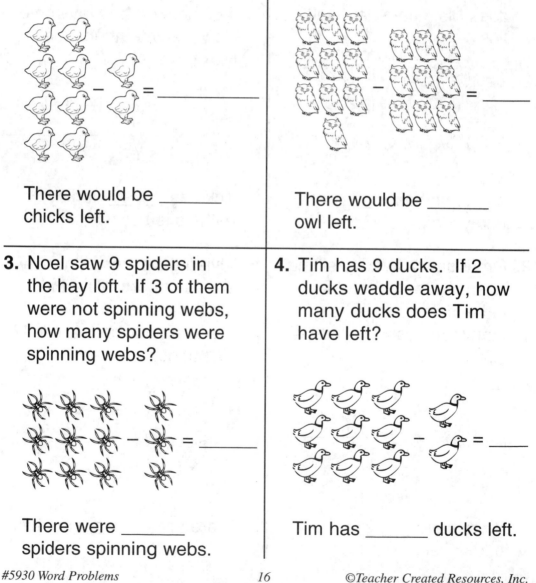

Word Problems #14

Directions: Solve the problems.

1. Tom has 3 toy cars. He gets 2 more for his birthday. How many toy cars does Tom have now? _____	**Show Your Work**
2. Sarah and Michelle are playing together. Kim and her sister come to play with them. How many girls are playing? _____	**Show Your Work**
3. Micah has 8 trading cards. He buys 5 more. How many trading cards does Micah have in all? _____	**Show Your Work**
4. Ryanna checked out 2 books from the school library. She checked out some more books from the city library. She has 7 books in all. How many books did she check out from the city library? _____	**Show Your Work**

Word Problems #15

Directions: Solve the problems. Show your work.

1. Stuart ate 10 candies. Glenn ate 3 candies. How many candies did they eat in all?

   They ate _____ candies in all.

2. Taylor counted 8 red roses and 6 white roses in the garden. How many roses did Taylor find in all?

   Taylor found _____ roses.

3. Yvonne collected 6 cans and 7 newspapers to take to the recycling center. How many items did Yvonne collect in all?

   Yvonne collected _____ items in all.

4. Lars is 7 years old. Lonnie is also 7 years old. If their ages were added together, how old would they be?

   They would be _____ years old.

Word Problems #16

Directions: Read and solve the word problems. Write and draw the solutions to the problems.

1. B. B. sorted his cards first. In the first group, he counted 5 baseball cards. In the second group, he counted 7 soccer cards.

   How many cards in all?____

2. J. C. sorted and counted his cards. In the first group, he counted 9 football cards. In the second group, he counted 6 basketball cards.

   How many cards in all?____

3. In his second group, B. B. counted 9 baseball cards and 8 soccer cards.

   How many cards in all?____

4. When J. C. counted his second group, he had 4 football cards and 10 basketball cards.

   How many cards in all?____

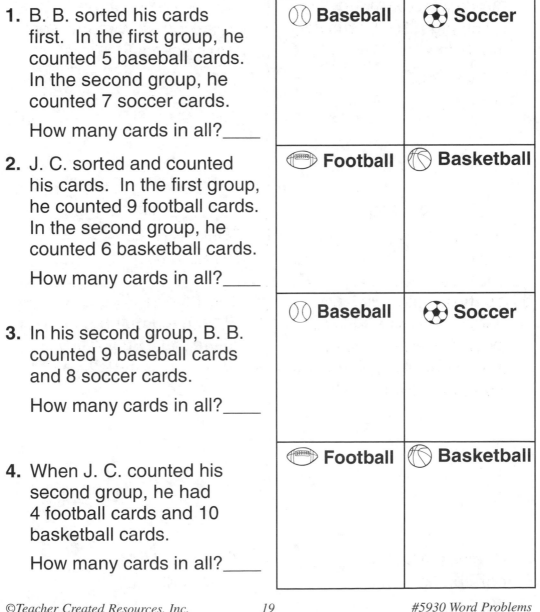

Word Problems #17

Directions: Solve the problems. Show your work.

1. Gwen has 10 pigs. If 3 ran into the barn, how many pigs did not run into the barn?

_____ pigs did not run into the barn.

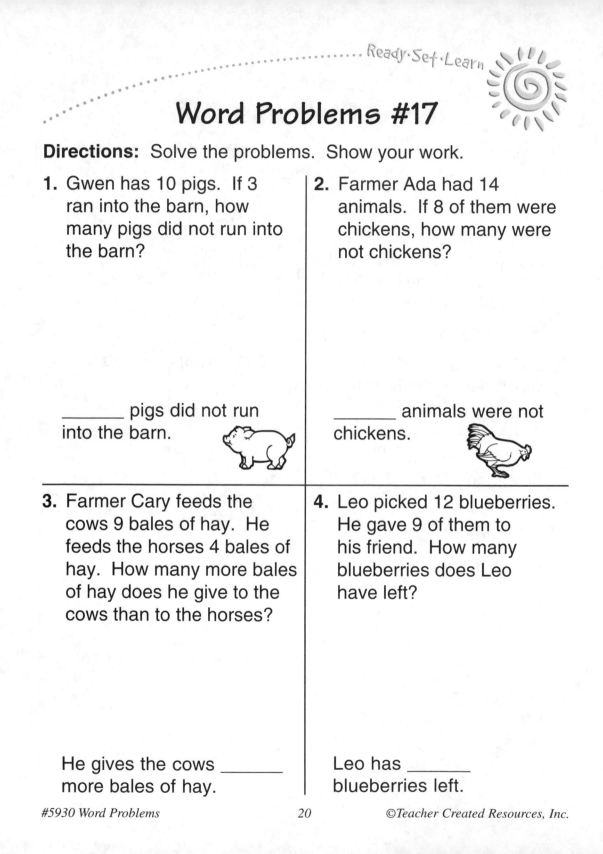

2. Farmer Ada had 14 animals. If 8 of them were chickens, how many were not chickens?

_____ animals were not chickens.

3. Farmer Cary feeds the cows 9 bales of hay. He feeds the horses 4 bales of hay. How many more bales of hay does he give to the cows than to the horses?

He gives the cows _____ more bales of hay.

4. Leo picked 12 blueberries. He gave 9 of them to his friend. How many blueberries does Leo have left?

Leo has _____ blueberries left.

Word Problems #18

Directions: Circle *add* or *subtract*.

1. I had 4 small green apples. Jamie gave me 1 red apple. How many apples do I have in all?

2. Gary found 1 yellow apple on the ground. He found 1 green apple on the fence. How many apples did Gary find in all?

add   **subtract**

add   **subtract**

3. Miranda bought 3 small apples and 1 large apple. How many apples did Miranda buy in all?

4. Barney picked 4 apples. He gave 2 of them away. How many apples does Barney have now?

add   **subtract**

add   **subtract**

Word Problems #19

Directions: Solve the problems.

1. There are 5 frogs. If 1 frog hops away, how many are left?

There are _____ frogs left.

2. There are 6 frogs. If 3 frogs hop away, how many are left?

There are _____ frogs left.

---

3. Jake went fishing. He caught 6 fish in the morning and 0 fish in the afternoon. How many fish did Jake catch in all?

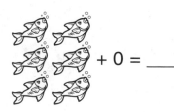

Jake caught _____ fish in all.

4. Ali caught 4 fish. She gave 3 to the Smith family. How many fish does Ali have left?

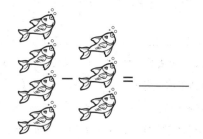

Ali has _____ fish left.

Word Problems #20

Directions: Solve the word problems below. Show your work with a number sentence or a picture on the right.

1. There are 4 pigs on the farm. Eight baby pigs are born. Now how many pigs are on the farm? _____	**Show Your Work**
2. There are 6 sheep in the barn. There are 7 sheep in the field. How many sheep are there altogether? _____	**Show Your Work**
3. There are 7 kittens on the farm. The farmer keeps one for each of his three children. He gives the rest away to his children's friends. How many kittens does he give away? _____	**Show Your Work**
4. There are 5 cows being milked. Seven cows are waiting to be milked. Six cows have already been milked. How many cows are on the farm in all? _____	**Show Your Work**

Word Problems #21

Directions: Solve the problems.

1. Amy made 1 scarecrow. Her friend gave her 8 more. How many scarecrows does Amy have in all?

$$1 + 8 = \underline{\hspace{3cm}}$$

Amy has _____ scarecrows in all.

2. Uncle Roberto made 10 paper turkeys. He gave away 5. How many paper turkeys does Uncle Roberto have left?

$$10 - 5 = \underline{\hspace{3cm}}$$

There are _____ paper turkeys left.

3. Mom placed 8 pumpkin pies on the windowsill. The dog ate 4 of them. How many pies are left?

$$8 - 4 = \underline{\hspace{3cm}}$$

There are _____ pies left.

4. Sue made 9 pumpkin pies for her family. Sue's family ate 2 pumpkin pies. How many pumpkin pies does Sue have left?

$$9 - 2 = \underline{\hspace{3cm}}$$

Sue has _____ pies left.

24

Word Problems #22

Directions: Solve the problems.

1. Ali planted 9 rows of corn on Thursday. He didn't plant any corn on Friday. How many rows of corn did Ali plant in all?

$$9 + 0 = \underline{\hspace{2cm}}$$

Ali planted _____ rows of corn in all.

2. Georgia had 7 ears of corn. She ate 4 ears of corn. How many ears did she have left?

$$7 - 4 = \underline{\hspace{2cm}}$$

She has _____ ears of corn.

3. Enrique made 10 corn tortillas. He gave 1 corn tortilla to Herman. How many tortillas does Enrique have left?

$$10 - 1 = \underline{\hspace{2cm}}$$

He has _____ tortillas left.

4. Lupe had 8 corn cakes. She ate 5 of them. How many corn cakes does Lupe have left?

$$8 - 5 = \underline{\hspace{2cm}}$$

Lupe has _____ corn cakes left.

Word Problems #23

Directions: Fill in the correct answer bubble.

1. There were 9 children playing outside. If 8 children went inside, how many children were still playing?

(A) 0   (B) 4

(C) 1   (D) 3

2. Saed has 5 books. He checked out 3 more books from the library. How many books does Saed have in all?

(A) 0   (B) 2

(C) 1   (D) 8

3. My teacher fixed 3 clocks yesterday and 7 clocks today. How many clocks did my teacher fix in all?

(A) 5   (B) 4

(C) 10   (D) 3

4. Larry stacked up 8 books. If 4 of the books fell over, how many books are left in the stack?

(A) 4   (B) 3

(C) 1   (D) 8

Word Problems #24

Directions: Solve the word problems below. Show your work in the space provided.

1. Marie has eight pieces of candy. She wants to share them equally with her friend Joanne. How many pieces of candy will each girl get? _____	**Show Your Work**
2. Sean wants to give three friends each five sticks of gum. Each pack of gum has five sticks of gum. How many packs of gum does Sean have to buy? _____	**Show Your Work**
3. Mary is three years older than her brother Tim. Tim is four years old. How old is Mary? _____	**Show Your Work**
4. It takes Emily 10 minutes to walk to school and 10 minutes to walk home from school. How many minutes does Emily spend walking to and from school each week? _____	**Show Your Work**

Word Problems #25

Directions: Solve the problems. Show your work.

1. Dareen caught 9 butterflies. Devin caught 3 butterflies. How many butterflies did they catch in all?

They caught _____ butterflies in all.

2. Justin made 7 pictures using crayons and 4 pictures using chalk. How many pictures did Justin make in all?

Justin made _____ pictures in all.

3. Ginger had 9 seashells. Now she has only 2. How many seashells did she lose?

Ginger lost _____ seashells.

4. Rosemary made 11 cookies. Her brother ate some. Now there are only 2 left. How many cookies did her brother eat?

He ate _____ cookies.

Word Problems #26

Directions: Solve the problems. Show your work.

1. Stacy had 12 pieces of candy. She gave 6 pieces to Raul. How many pieces of candy does Stacy have left?

Stacy has _____ pieces left.

2. Bea has 6 candles. She buys 5 more. How many candles does Bea now have?

Bea has _____ candles.

3. Manuel made 11 cakes. He sold 6 at the fair. How many cakes does Manuel have left?

Manuel has _____ cakes left.

4. Omar can play 9 songs on his guitar. He has already played 3 songs. How many more songs can Omar play?

Omar can play _____ more songs.

Word Problems #27

Directions: Solve the problems. Show your work.

1. Dave ate 3 doughnuts for breakfast. He ate 4 more doughnuts for snack. How many doughnuts did Dave eat in all?

Dave ate _____ doughnuts in all.

2. Hector had 10 apples. He ate 2. How many are left?

_____ apples left.

3. Dana made 4 sandwiches. Then she made 6 more. How many sandwiches did Dana make in all?

Dana made _____ sandwiches in all.

4. Solomon had 10 eggs. His dog ate 4 of them. How many eggs does Solomon have left?

Solomon has _____ eggs left.

Word Problems #28

Directions: Solve the problems. Write the answers on the lines provided.

1. John's magnet held 3 paper clips.
   Sarah's magnet held 7 paper clips.
   How many more paper clips does
   Sarah's magnet hold? _____

2. Chang used his magnet to pick up 2 keys,
   1 paper clip, and 4 pins.
   How many items were picked up altogether? _____

3. Ashley had 9 magnets.
   She gave 2 magnets to Jodi.
   She gave 1 magnet to Seth.
   How many magnets does Ashley still have? _____

4. David has 12 magnets.
   Tomeka has 7 magnets.
   How many more magnets does David have? _____

5. A ring magnet attracted 9 pins.
   A bar magnet attracted 8 pins.
   How many pins were attracted altogether? _____

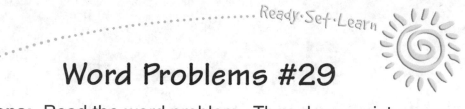

Word Problems #29

Directions: Read the word problem. Then draw a picture on each plate to show how you solved the problem.

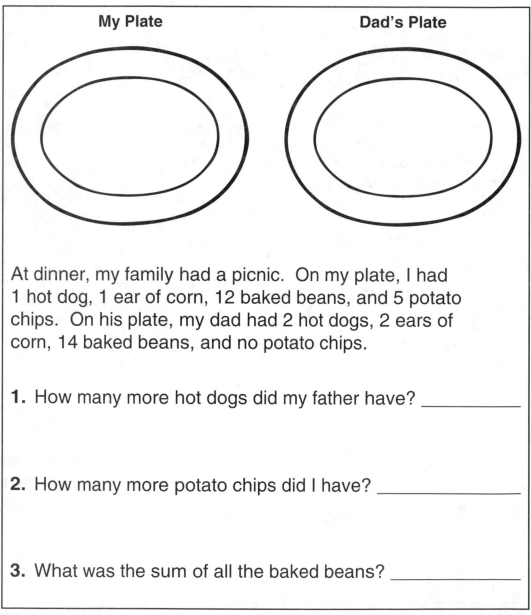

At dinner, my family had a picnic. On my plate, I had 1 hot dog, 1 ear of corn, 12 baked beans, and 5 potato chips. On his plate, my dad had 2 hot dogs, 2 ears of corn, 14 baked beans, and no potato chips.

1. How many more hot dogs did my father have? _____

2. How many more potato chips did I have? _____

3. What was the sum of all the baked beans? _____

Word Problems #30

Directions: Use the target board below to solve the problems.

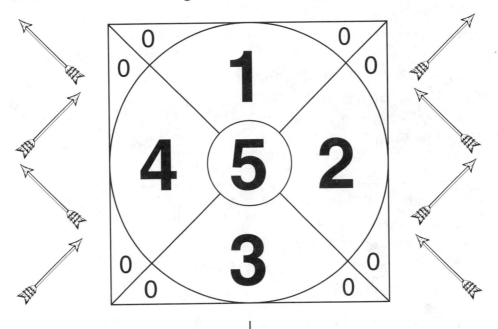

1. Robin shot two arrows for a total of 5 points. The first arrow hit the 0. What was the other number that Robin hit?

   Robin hit the _____.

2. Maid Marion shot two arrows for a total of 3 points. The first arrow hit the 2. What was the other number that Maid Marion hit?

   Maid Marion hit the _____.

3. Little John shot two arrows for a total of 10 points. The first arrow hit the 5. What was the other number that Little John hit?

   Little John hit the _____.

4. Friar Tuck shot two arrows for a total of 0 points. What were the two numbers that Friar Tuck hit?

   Friar Tuck hit the _____ and the _____.

Ready·Set·Learn

Word Problems #31

Directions: Solve the problems below. Show your work in the space provided.

1. Three children had a race at recess. Tony came in last. Sarah came in after Mark. Who came in first? Who came in second? Who came in third? _____	**Show Your Work**
2. Jose invited five children to his birthday party. He wants to give each child two balloons, including himself. How many balloons does Jose need to buy? _____	**Show Your Work**
3. Maurice is going to buy lunch at school on Tuesday. He will bring his lunch on all other school days. How many days must he pack his lunch? _____	**Show Your Work**
4. Brenda gets five cents for each bottle she recycles. How much money will she earn if she recycles 10 bottles? _____	**Show Your Work**

Word Problems #32

Directions: Solve the problems.

1. Frank bought 10 tickets. A friend gave him 15 more. How many tickets does Frank have in all?

$$10 \\ +15$$

Frank has _____ tickets in all.

2. Mr. Simons caught 30 fish in the morning and 40 fish in the afternoon. How many fish did he catch in all?

$$30 \\ +40$$

Mr. Simons caught _____ fish in all.

3. Shannon made 14 baskets in the first game and 20 baskets in the second game. How many baskets did Shannon make in all?

$$14 \\ +20$$

Shannon made _____ baskets in all.

4. Dean had a necktie with 31 red dots and 42 blue dots. How many dots in all did Dean have on his tie?

$$31 \\ +42$$

Dean had _____ dots in all.

Word Problems #33

Directions: Solve the problems. Show your work.

1. Maria had 45 stamps in her collection. Her aunt gave her 54 more. How many stamps does Maria have in all?

$$+ \rule{3cm}{0.4pt}$$

Maria has _____ stamps in all.

2. Ferdinand planted 60 yellow tulips and 10 pink tulips. How many tulips did Ferdinand plant in all?

$$+ \rule{3cm}{0.4pt}$$

Ferdinand planted _____ tulips in all.

3. Mickey has 70 baseball cards and 20 football cards. How many cards does Mickey have in all?

$$+ \rule{3cm}{0.4pt}$$

Mickey has _____ cards in all.

4. My first cookie had 15 chocolate chips in it. My second cookie had 21 chocolate chips in it. How many chocolate chips were there in all?

$$+ \rule{3cm}{0.4pt}$$

There were _____ chocolate chips in all.

Word Problems #34

Directions: Solve the problems. Show your work

1. Lisa had 73 cookies. She sold 12 of them. How many cookies does she have left?

$$73$$
$$-12$$

Lisa has _____ cookies left.

2. Tim's dog had 26 fleas. 13 of them jumped off. How many fleas are left on Tim's dog?

$$26$$
$$-13$$

Tim's dog has _____ fleas left.

3. Buster looked in his toy box and found 87 marbles. He gave 10 to Tom. How many marbles does Buster have left?

$$87$$
$$-10$$

Buster has _____ marbles left.

4. Mark had 35 pairs of white socks. He lost 13 pairs of white socks on vacation. How many pairs of white socks does Mark have left?

$$35$$
$$-13$$

Mark has _____ pairs of white socks left.

Word Problems #35

Directions: Fill in the correct answer bubble.

1. The children made 55 blueberry pancakes and 41 buttermilk pancakes. How many pancakes did they make in all?

   (A) 14   (B) 86

   (C) 13   (D) 96

2. There are 99 days in winter. If 15 days have passed, how many more days of winter are left?

   (A) 84   (B) 114

   (C) 74   (D) 48

3. My cousin has 63 coins in his piggy bank. I have 21 coins in my piggy bank. How many coins do we have in all?

   (A) 84   (B) 86

   (C) 42   (D) 48

4. At the pie-eating contest, there were 67 pies. Leslie's team ate 31 pies. How many pies were left?

   (A) 84   (B) 9

   (C) 26   (D) 36

38

Word Problems #36

Directions: Circle *add* or *subtract*.

1. Polly counted 49 butterflies. If 36 of them flew away, how many are left?

add

subtract

2. William had 71 red spots on one arm and 28 red spots on the other arm. How many spots did he have in all?

add

subtract

3. Kim picked 27 flowers. If 16 wilted on the way home, how many are still fresh?

add

subtract

4. Tracy had 38 letters. She mailed 24 of them. How many are left?

add

subtract

Word Problems #37

Directions: Use the money chart to help you solve the problems.

1¢	5¢	10¢	25¢

1. Jerome has 1 nickel in his pocket. How much money does Jerome have?

   Circle the answer.

   5¢   15¢   25¢

2. C.J. has 1 quarter in her pocket. How much money does C.J. have?

   Circle the answer.

   5¢   10¢   25¢

3. Mabel has two pockets. In one pocket she has 1 nickel. In the other pocket she has 1 dime. How much money does Mabel have?

   Circle the answer.

   5¢   15¢   25¢

4. Neil has two pockets, too. In one pocket he has 1 nickel. In the other pocket he has another nickel. How much money does Neil have?

   Circle the answer.

   5¢   10¢   25¢

40

Word Problems #38

Directions: Use the money chart to help you solve the problems.

1¢	5¢	10¢	25¢

1. Xavier found 6¢ in his shirt pocket and 3¢ in his jacket pocket. How much money did Xavier find in all?

6¢ + 3¢ = _____ ¢

Xavier found _____¢.

2. Maria had 5¢ in her piggy bank and 3¢ in her purse. How much money did Maria have in all?

5¢ + 3¢ = _____ ¢

Maria has _____¢ .

3. I have 2 coins that make exactly 6¢. One of the coins is a nickel. What is the other coin?

The other coin is a

_____.

4. I have 2 coins that make exactly 10¢. Both of the coins are the same. What are the two coins that I have?

The two coins are both

_____.

Word Problems #39

Directions: Use the money chart to help you solve the problems.

1¢	**5¢**	**10¢**	**25¢**

1. Stephanie had 18¢. She spent 10¢ on an ice cream cone. How much money does Stephanie have left?

$$
\begin{array}{r}
18¢ \\
- \ 10¢ \\
\hline
\end{array}
$$

Stephanie has _____ ¢ left.

2. Tyrone has 36¢. He bought a model car for 25¢. How much money does Tyrone have left?

$$
\begin{array}{r}
36¢ \\
- \ 25¢ \\
\hline
\end{array}
$$

Tyrone has _____ ¢ left.

3. Imani had 20¢. She spent 10¢ on an ice cream cone. How much money does Imani have left?

$$
\begin{array}{r}
20¢ \\
- \ 10¢ \\
\hline
\end{array}
$$

Imani had _____ ¢ left.

4. Esperanza had 2 quarters and 3 pennies. She bought a toy for 21¢. How much money did she have left?

$$
\begin{array}{r}
¢ \\
- \quad ¢ \\
\hline
\end{array}
$$

Esperanza had _____ ¢ left.

42

Word Problems #40

Directions: Use the money chart to help you solve the problems.

1¢	5¢	10¢	25¢

1. Mary had 43¢. She spent 33¢ on an eraser. How much money does Mary have left?

   _____
   _____

   Mary has _____ ¢ left.

2. Rosa has 72¢. She bought a book for 50¢. How much money does Rosa have left?

   _____
   _____

   Rosa has _____ ¢ left.

3. Stephanie had 57¢. She spent 42¢ on a pack of gum. How much money does Stephanie have left?

   _____
   _____

   Stephanie has ____ ¢ left.

4. Craig had 3 quarters and 4 pennies. He bought a toy for 51¢. How much money did he have left?

   _____
   _____

   Craig had _____ ¢ left.

Word Problems #41

Directions: Fill in the correct answer bubble.

1. Herb had 26¢. He spent 13¢ buying a candy bar. How much money does Herb have left?

(A) 39¢   (B) 12¢

(C) 19¢   (D) 13¢

2. Betty had 45¢ in one pocket and 33¢ in another pocket. How much money does Betty have?

(A) 12¢   (B) 78¢

(C) 68¢   (D) 11¢

3. Dale had 57¢. He found 12¢ in his pocket. How much money does Dale have?

(A) 55¢   (B) 69¢

(C) 45¢   (D) 49¢

4. Fay had 89¢. She spent 70¢ buying a candy bar. How much money does Fay have left?

(A) 15¢   (B) 18¢

(C) 19¢   (D) 20¢

Word Problems #42

1. Raul takes a 1-hour nap each day. He fell asleep at 1:00. What time does Raul wake up?

Show the time on the clock.

2. Fran went to the 3:00 movie. The movie was 2 hours long. What time did the movie end?

Show the time on the clock.

3. Phil eats dinner at 8:00 P.M. and goes to bed 1/2 hour later. What time does Phil go to bed?

Show the time on the clock.

4. Marianne gets up at 7:00 A.M. and goes to school 1/2 hour after she gets up. What time does she go to school?

Show the time on the clock.

Word Problems #43

1. The play began at 6:00 and lasted 1/2 hour. What time did the play end?

Show the time and write it.

_____ : _____

2. The school bus picked us up at 2:00. The bus ride took 1/2 hour. What time did we get home?

Show the time and write it.

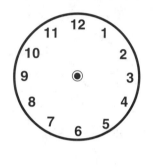

_____ : _____

3. We went to the park at 4:00. We played for 1/2 hour. What time did we leave the park?

Show the time and write it.

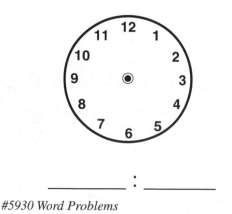

_____ : _____

4. The baby fell asleep at 9:00 and napped for 1/2 hour. What time did the baby wake up?

Show the time and write it.

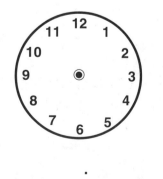

_____ : _____

Word Problems #44

Directions: Use the shapes to solve the problem.

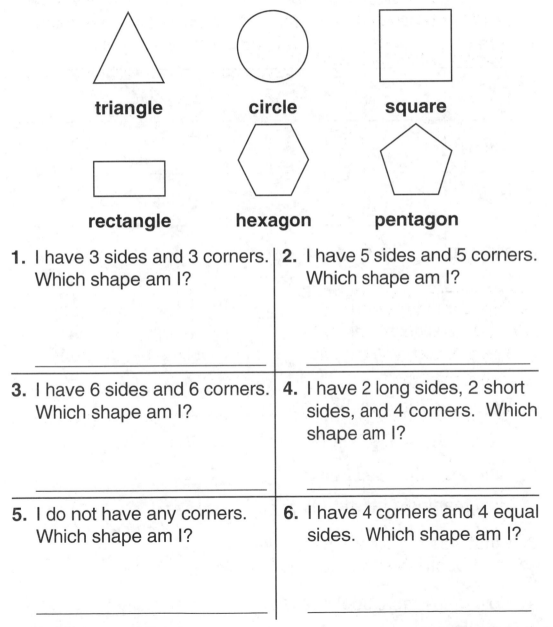

triangle   circle   square

rectangle hexagon pentagon

1. I have 3 sides and 3 corners. Which shape am I?

_____

2. I have 5 sides and 5 corners. Which shape am I?

_____

3. I have 6 sides and 6 corners. Which shape am I?

_____

4. I have 2 long sides, 2 short sides, and 4 corners. Which shape am I?

_____

5. I do not have any corners. Which shape am I?

_____

6. I have 4 corners and 4 equal sides. Which shape am I?

_____

Word Problems #45

Directions: Cory, Josh, Kelly, and Natasha were supposed to read one book each day for a week. The *pictograph* below shows how many they each read. The *key* shows that each picture of a book represents one book.

Cory	📖 📖 📖 📖 📖 📖
Josh	📖 📖 📖 📖
Kelly	📖 📖 📖 📖 📖
Natasha	📖 📖 📖 📖 📖 📖 📖

KEY
📖 = 1 book

1. Who read the most books? _____

How many did he/she read? _____

2. Who read the least books? _____

How many did he/she read? _____

3. What was the difference between the
most books and the least books read? _____

4. How many more books did Cory read than Kelly? _____

48

Word Problems #46

Directions: Fill in the correct answer bubble.

1. I am greater than 10 and less than 14. I am an even number. What number am I?

(A) 14 (B) 10

(C) 11 (D) 12

2. I am greater than 15 and less than 25. When you count by tens you say my name. What number am I?

(A) 20 (B) 4

(C) 1 (D) 30

3. I am an even number. I am greater than 30 and less than 50. When you count by tens you say my name. What number am I?

(A) 35 (B) 40

(C) 45 (D) 50

4. I am an odd number. I am greater than 80 and less than 90. When you count by fives you say my name. What number am I?

(A) 80 (B) 85

(C) 90 (D) 98

Word Problems #47

Directions: Solve each word problem and write your answer.

1. Sara has 7 cats and Renee has 8 cats. How many cats do the two girls have combined?

The girls have _____cats.

2. Ellie opened 4 gifts from her parents, 2 gifts from her grandparents, and 1 gift from her older brother. How many gifts did Ellie open in all?

Ellie opened _____ gifts.

3. Pete picked 8 apples from an apple tree. Jason picked 4 more than Pete. How many apples did Jason pick?

Jason picked _____ apples.

4. Joe bought a package of socks. There were 2 gray socks, 4 white socks, and 2 black socks. How many total socks were in the package?

There were _____ socks in the package.

Word Problems #48

Directions: Solve each word problem and write your answer.

1. At the beach, Artie found 9 small shells and 4 large shells. How many shells did Artie find in all? Artie found _____ shells.	**2.** Mary drew 2 cubes, 3 triangles, and 6 rectangles. How many total shapes did Mary draw in all? Mary drew _____ shapes.
3. Clint counted 6 horses, 4 cows, and a goat in the field. How many total animals did Clint count? Clint counted _____ animals.	**4.** Michael has 5 green shirts, 3 yellow shirts, and 2 red shirts in his suitcase. How many total shirts does Michael have? Michael has _____ shirts.

Word Problems #49

Directions: Solve each word problem and write your answer.

1. Last season, Freddy hit 9 home runs and Kurt hit 6. How many more home runs did Freddy hit than Kurt? Freddy hit _____ more home runs.	2. Archie gets $10 in allowance from his parents. This week, he gave his little brother $2 to buy some candy. How much of this week's allowance does Archie have left? Artie has _____ left.
3. Twelve children climbed a rope ladder to a tree house. Five people climbed back down. How many people are still in the tree house? _____ children are still in the tree house.	4. Marco and Shelly bought 12 donuts. Marco ate 3 and Shelly ate 1. They gave the rest to their friends. How many donuts did they give to their friends? They gave _____ donuts to their friends.

Word Problems #50

Directions: Solve each word problem and write your answer.

1. Sam scored 8 points in the basketball game yesterday. Kimberly scored 6 more points than Sam. How many points did Kimberly score? Kimberly scored _____ points.	2. Mandy has 10 blue ribbons for swimming. Peggy has 7 blue ribbons for swimming. How many more blue ribbons does Mandy have? Mandy has _____ more blue ribbons.
3. Dave and Kathy wanted to share 6 pieces of pizza. How many pieces will each of them get? Each will get _____ pieces.	4. Mike has 8 letters to mail, but he only has 5 stamps. How many more stamps does he need to buy? He needs to buy _____ more stamps.

Word Problems #51

Directions: Solve each word problem and write your answer.

---

1. Sal made 16 pizzas. He sold 9 of them. How many pizzas does Sal still have?

Sal has _____ pizzas left to sell.

2. Paul sells hats. He started the day with 14 hats. Now he only has 1 left. How many hats did Paul sell?

Paul sold _____ hats.

---

3. Jan put 17 cookies in a box. She took 6 out. How many cookies are in the box?

_____ cookies are in the box.

4. Daisy drew 12 red hearts. Then she drew 8 purple hearts. How many hearts did Daisy draw in all?

Daisy drew _____ hearts.

Word Problems #52

Ready·Set·Learn

Directions: Solve each word problem and write your answer.

---

1. Matt brought 18 cupcakes to school. Fifteen were eaten. How many cupcakes are left?

_____ cupcakes are left.

---

2. Jake found 14 keys in his desk drawer. Seven of the keys are gold and the rest are silver. How many keys are silver?

_____ keys are silver.

---

3. Angela baked 2 apple pies. Each pie had 5 slices. How many slices of apple pie were there in all?

There were _____ slices of apple pie.

---

4. Jimmy bought 2 baseball cards for $1. How much money will 4 baseball cards cost?

Four baseball cards will cost _____.

Word Problems #53

Directions: Solve each word problem and write your answer.

1. Linda gave 3 pencils to Jake and 2 pencils to Cindy. Linda now has 1 pencil left. How many pencils did Linda have at the beginning? Linda had _____ pencils at the beginning.	**2.** Diana invited 16 friends to her birthday party. Six friends did not come to the party. How many friends came to Diana's birthday party? _____ friends came to Diana's party.
3. Pedro bought 6 pairs of socks. There are 2 socks in each pair. How many total socks did Pedro buy? Pedro bought _____ socks.	**4.** Mary has 5 dolls. Cindy has some dolls, also. Together, Mary and Cindy have 9 dolls. How many dolls does Cindy have? Cindy has _____ dolls.

Word Problems #54

Directions: Solve each word problem and write your answer.

---

1. Jacqueline has 7 lollipops in a bag. Three of the lollipops are cherry-flavored. The rest of the lollipops are grape. How many of the lollipops are grape?

_____ lollipops are grape.

---

2. Margo has 5 fish and 2 birds. Justin has 6 fish and 1 cat. How many fish do Margo and Justin have in all?

Margo and Justin have _____ fish.

---

3. Yolanda picked 7 roses yesterday. Today, Yolanda picked 12 roses. How many more roses did Yolanda pick today than yesterday?

Yolanda picked _____ more roses.

---

4. Brandy did 15 somersaults. Her friend Ashley did 9 fewer somersaults than Brandy did. How many somersaults did Ashley do?

Ashley did _____ somersaults.

Word Problems #55

Directions: Solve each word problem and write your answer.

---

1. A tricycle has 3 wheels and 1 seat. How many wheels and seats are there all together on 3 tricycles?

There are _____ wheels and _____ seats.

2. Meg needs to read 25 pages for homework. She has already read 11 pages. How many more pages does she need to read?

Meg needs to read _____ more pages.

---

3. Dad has 23 neckties. He gave away 11 of them. How many ties does Dad now have?

Dad has _____ ties left.

4. Cecilia ran 12 miles yesterday and 9 miles today. How many miles did Cecilia run in all?

Cecilia ran _____ miles.

Word Problems #56

Directions: Solve each word problem and write your answer.

---

1. Dwight had 15 marbles. His friend Andy gave him 15 more. How many marbles does Dwight now have?

Dwight has _____ marbles.

2. Sabrina made 34 necklaces during summer break. She gave 21 of those necklaces to her friends. She kept the rest. How many necklaces did Sabrina keep for herself?

Sabrina kept _____ necklaces for herself.

---

3. Callie has 3 jars. There are 10 buttons in each jar. How many buttons does Callie have altogether?

Callie has _____ buttons.

4. There are 29 ducks swimming in a pond. Sixteen of the ducks are gray and the rest are white. How many of the ducks are white?

There are _____ white ducks in the pond.

Word Problems #57

Directions: Solve each word problem and write your answer.

1. There are 14 crayons in a package. How many crayons are there in 2 packages? There are _____ crayons.	**2.** There are 12 eggs in a dozen. How many eggs are there in 3 dozen? There are _____ eggs.
3. Sandra, Beth, and Kenny each picked 6 roses. How many roses did they pick altogether? They picked _____ roses.	**4.** Jim bought lunch 4 times this week. Each lunch cost $6.00. How much did Jim spend this week on lunch? Jim spent _____ on lunch.

Answer Key

Page 4
1. 15 bags
2. 13 popsicles
3. 6 more cans
4. 17 jars

Page 5
1. 12   3. 5   5. 25
2. 21   4. 16   6. 31

Page 6
1. 8¢ − 4¢ = 4¢
2. 5¢ − 5¢ = 0¢
3. 8¢ − 3¢ = 5¢
4. 9¢ − 5¢ = 4¢
5. 4¢ − 2¢ = 2¢
6. 7¢ − 6¢ = 1¢

Page 7
1. 5   3. 5
2. 6   4. 7

Page 8
1. 7   3. 4
2. 9   4. 6

Page 9
1. 6   3. 5
2. 4   4. 6

Page 10
1. 3   3. 6
2. 5   4. 1

Page 11
1. 2 + 3 = 5   3. 4 + 3 = 7
2. 5 + 4 = 9

Page 12
1. 9   3. 8
2. 9   4. 5

Page 13
1. 7   3. 8
2. 9   4. 9

Page 14
1. 7 − 3 = 4   3. 5 − 2 = 3
2. 6 − 2 = 4   4. 8 − 6 = 2

Page 15
1. 2   3. 4
2. 3   4. 7

Page 16
1. 6   3. 6
2. 1   4. 7

Page 17
1. 3 + 2 = 5
2. 2 + 2 = 4
3. 8 + 5 = 13
4. 7 − 2 = 5

Page 18
1. 10 + 3 = 13
2. 8 + 6 = 14
3. 6 + 7 = 13
4. 7 + 7 = 14

Page 19
1. 12   3. 17
2. 15   4. 14

Page 20
1. 7   3. 5
2. 6   4. 3

Page 21
1. add   3. add
2. add   4. subtract

Page 22
1. 4   3. 6
2. 3   4. 1

Page 23
1. 12   3. 4
2. 13   4. 18

Page 24
1. 9   3. 4
2. 5   4. 7

Page 25
1. 9   3. 9
2. 3   4. 3

Page 26
1. C   3. C
2. D   4. A

Page 27
1. 4 pieces
2. 3 packs
3. 7 years old
4. 100 minutes

Page 28
1. 12   3. 7
2. 11   4. 9

Page 29
1. 6   3. 5
2. 11   4. 6

Page 30
1. 7   3. 10
2. 8   4. 6

Page 31
1. 4   4. 5
2. 7   5. 17
3. 6

Page 32
1. 1
2. 5
3. 26

Page 33
1. 5   3. 5
2. 1   4. 0, 0

Answer Key *(cont.)*

Page 34
1. Mark, Sarah, Tony
2. 12
3. 4
4. 50 cents

Page 35
1. 25   3. 34
2. 70   4. 73

Page 36
1. 99   3. 90
2. 70   4. 36

Page 37
1. 61   3. 77
2. 13   4. 22

Page 38
1. D   3. A
2. A   4. D

Page 39
1. subtract   3. subtract
2. add   4. subtract

Page 40
1. 5¢   3. 15¢
2. 25¢   4. 10¢

Page 41
1. 9   3. penny
2. 8   4. nickels

Page 42
1. 8   3. 10
2. 11   4. 32

Page 43
1. 10   3. 15
2. 22   4. 28

Page 44
1. D   3. B
2. B   4. C

Page 45
1. 2:00   3. 8:30
2. 5:00   4. 7:30

Page 46
1. 6:30   3. 4:30
2. 2:30   4. 9:30

Page 47
1. triangle
2. pentagon
3. hexagon
4. rectangle
5. circle
6. square

Page 48
1. Natasha, 7
2. Josh, 4
3. 3 books
4. 1 book

Page 49
1. D   3. B
2. A   4. B

Page 50
1. 15   3. 12
2. 7   4. 8

Page 51
1. 13   3. 11
2. 11   4. 10

Page 52
1. 3   3. 7
2. $8   4. 8

Page 53
1. 14
2. 3
3. 3
4. 3

Page 54
1. 7
2. 13
3. 11
4. 20

Page 55
1. 3
2. 7
3. 10
4. $2

Page 56
1. 6
2. 10
3. 12
4. 4

Page 57
1. 4
2. 11
3. 5
4. 6

Page 58
1. 9 wheels, 3 seats
2. 14
3. 12
4. 21

Page 59
1. 30
2. 13
3. 30
4. 13

Page 60
1. 28
2. 36
3. 18
4. $24